Betty Gets Ready...
for the Doctor

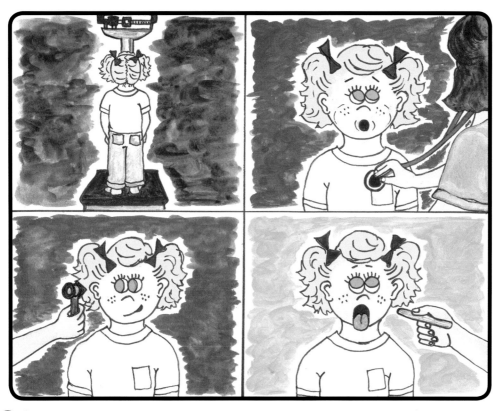

Written and Illustrated by Kathi Greene

AuthorHouse™
1663 Liberty Drive
Bloomington, IN 47403
www.authorhouse.com
Phone: 1 (833) 262-8899

Because of the dynamic nature of the Internet, any web addresses or links contained in this book may have changed
since publication and may no longer be valid. The views expressed in this work are solely those of the author and do not
necessarily reflect the views of the publisher, and the publisher hereby disclaims any responsibility for them.

Any people depicted in stock imagery provided by Getty Images are models,
and such images are being used for illustrative purposes only.
Certain stock imagery © Getty Images.

This book is printed on acid-free paper.

ISBN: 978-1-4389-4936-9 (sc)

Library of Congress Control Number: 2009902851

Print information available on the last page.

Published by AuthorHouse 09/23/2020

authorHOUSE®

Betty gets ready,
to the doctor she goes.
She wants to get ready
from her head to her toes.

The doctor must check
each muscle and bone,
to make sure she's healthy,
to make sure she's grown.

So as Betty gets ready,
she thinks for a bit.
How should Betty get ready
for her doctor visit?

She must be all clean
and smell really sweet,

scrub her cheeks and her chin,
and the dirt from her feet.

"Should I change my clothes too?"
Betty says as she sees
the spills on her play shirt
and the holes in her knees.

"I think wearing clean clothes
is the right thing to do.
I'll find something less dirty,
But where's my left shoe?"

To help Betty get ready
her mom's placed on the chair
a white shirt, some blue jeans,
and some clean underwear.

"Now I'm all clean!"
Betty says with a smile.
"But I must brush my teeth,
for it's been quite a while!"

For she knows that the doctor
must take a long look,
in her mouth, at her tonsils,
and in every small nook.

The doctor will weigh her
and listen to her lungs,
check her ears and her eyes,
look for bumps on her tongue.

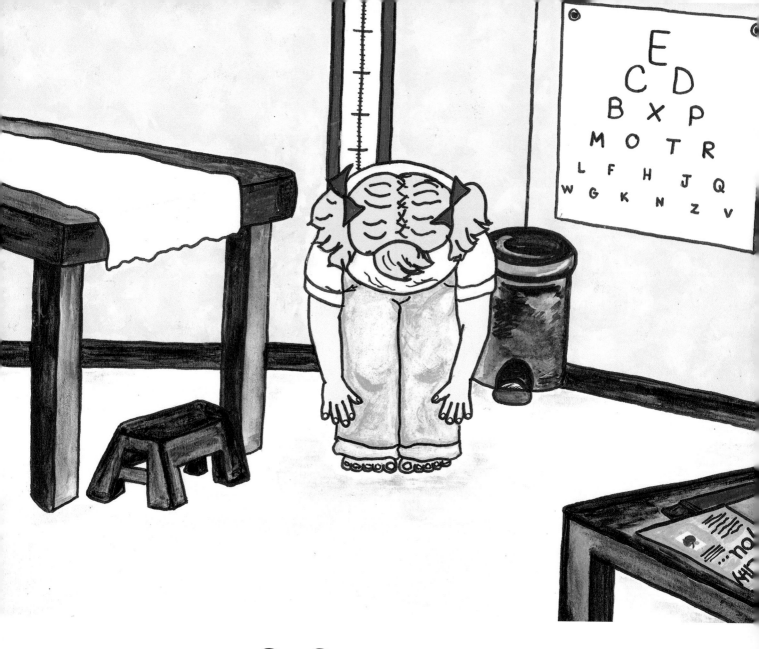

Can I see every letter?
Can I hear every sound?
Does my backbone look straight
when I reach for the ground?

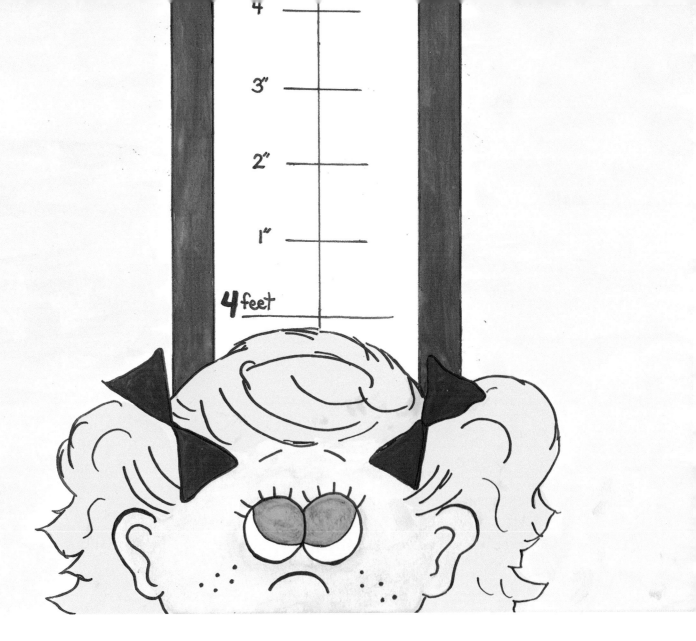

I'm sure I'll be measured
to see if I'm tall.
I'll stand straight and so still
with my back to the wall.

Will they measure me with shoes on?
Or will bare feet quite do?
Good thing I have clean socks,
"But where's that left shoe?"

I must tell the doctor
all the things that I do,
to be healthy and happy
and so very smart too!

I drink all my milk,
eat my peas off the plate,
and I make sure my bedtime
is never too late.

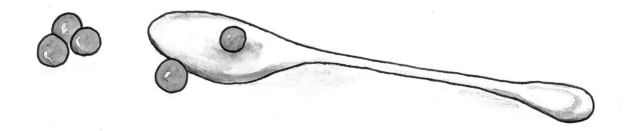

The computer and TV
I use just for short times.
I'd rather read books
that have stories and rhymes.

It is very important
that my brain's growing too.
So I read and I play,
"Oh there's my left shoe!"

When I'm riding my bike,
I wear my helmet on my head,
but if I ride in the car,
I buckle my seatbelt instead.

These are all of the things
that Betty must do
to keep growing, stay healthy,
and be very safe too!

Now, as Betty gets ready
she remembers one thing,
she may need a shot
so her bear she must bring.

The shot makes her healthy,
keeps her from getting too sick,
but her bear gives her comfort
when she feels that prick.

Betty's almost all ready
for her checkup today,
and if she is good,
the doctor might say ...

"Here's a sticker, Miss Betty.
Your visit was grand!
You're the healthiest kid
in the entire land!"

Now Betty is ready
for the doctor, you see.
When Betty gets ready,
she's as ready as can be!

Printed in the United States
By Bookmasters